Words Remembered in Time

Brandon "Saker" Doyle

authorHOUSE®

AuthorHouse™
1663 Liberty Drive
Bloomington, IN 47403
www.authorhouse.com
Phone: 1-800-839-8640

Published by AuthorHouse   05/25/2012

ISBN: 978-1-4685-8260-4 (sc)
ISBN: 978-1-4685-8259-8 (e)

Contents

Pain

Through Ends and Outs
Troubles and Pain
There is no doubt my power shall reign
Though years my pass and warriors my fall
My chosen few will not change at all
I'm just a lost soul seeking wisdom from the trees
To get me where I am destined to be
To decipher these drawings that are given to me, these
Drawings from the future and writing from the past is the only thing
That help me last As I move through the shadows and fight through the sun
As one day ends that's just another lesson done . . . .
Lessons come fast but are not completed at once
So the many lessons accomplished over one life time
Can never be measured at its full potential
This proves one thing playing catch-up with time is a game you shall
always lose
Even though time cannot be mastered but only be changed
One thing is for certain my power shall reign
Through altered time and deleted space my friends and my family fuel my faith
My body may die but my soul shall remain in its ghostly shape my wisdom
It reframes and with this wisdom I shall rise from the ashes like a Phoenix
Using its resurrection magic and when I arise my warriors will too
The pain will be gone and the troubles will to and like I said
My warriors will not have changed they will look like they did
Before this High time of change . . . .
With years gone by and friends have passed their souls are with me on my
final task
And when this task is completed their souls must pass to a higher place
Away from this troubled realm but because of my curse I am stuck in this realm
That is filled with anger and hate but with this curse you will

Never see my body or my soul leave this realm where I hate to be but
instead I will rise like a Phoenix
From the ashes because this curse has its hands
Clutched around me for eternity . . . .

Painfully true,
Saker

Mind Wondering

Sorrow is over
    Tomorrow is a new day
  How do we get there, do we just run to it?
            Or do our minds transport us through time and
  Space just to get us to the next time or place
        This so called tomorrow.
                Or is tomorrow just another yesterday just
            Being repeated and recycled in our minds
    Stuck in an everlasting eternity doomed to recycle
  Their minds and show no further progress
                Still to be figured out like an old rubrics cube
        As I ponder these thoughts while
      Looking out unto the world I stare into to my
  Hour glass watching as each grain fall gracefully
        Into place until it all has stopped
    Waiting to be tilted back over
              Watching this traps
      In a daze, it thinks I'm crazy
    Like the sun but I am not I am just nocturnal
  Up all night dream all day like a river my mind is always at play
  And yet I really have to say I don't sleep I slip
Into these coded messages or so called dreams that need to be interpreted
But reveal nothing more than just a little more about you
Yet we take it for granted that our body has figured something out
  We think we know it all but we do not
We live I a society that does not sleep much or does not sleep
Long enough to be able to understand these dreams . . .
They
    WORK
            LIVE
        , DESTORY
            , DRINK
                , DO DRUGS
                    , and SMOKE
        All these are just distractions in this world to
Keep you from finding yourself, to keep you from finding
Your hour glass to star into and think about the wonders of this world
                        Painfully True,
                        Saker

2   *Brandon "Saker" Doyle*

Love

I was told by someone wise that
Some people, only love with their hearts. But others,
Love passed their heart and into their soul, for
Those who love past their hearts and into their soul will
Love forever uncontested and
Unchanged, faithful forever more . . .
But most people don't understand FOREVER . . .
Forever not meaning a life time but
Forever meaning eternity as in for many lives to come
Or as in beyond the normal capacity of a human to love,
I don't know about u but I chose to love beyond all levels of
The human constraints . . . I plan on loving with my soul into eternity
Bound by that one thing I believe in
FAITH . . . .

Painfully True,
Saker

My Name

Saker . . . Soul. Among. Klouded. Ententions. of Revenge . . .
　　But what is revenge
　　　The blind showing of rage towards others . . .
No not of Revenge, of Remorse
　　But I was told not to be sorry for anything I do
　　　　So no not of Remorse, of rejoice
　　　　　　But if I Rejoice then I'm showing that I am too happy
　　Be happy in moderation
　　　　　　So not of Rejoice but of Redemption
　　　　　　To prove one's self to others
　　　　　　　　But one should never truly care what everyone else thinks
So not of Redemption but of Reconciliation yes . . .
　　Reconciliation to make everything around me better
　　　　　　And to stop the fight between my mind and soul
　　　　　　So that this lost soul may be found
　　　　　　　　But until that day I will
　　　　　　　　Remain a Soul Among Klouded Ententions
　　　　　　　　of Reconciliation . . .
　　　　　　　　　　A SAKER forevermore . . . .
　　　　　　　　　　　　Painfully True,
　　　　　　　　　　　　SAKER

Brandon "Saker" Doyle

Rant #1

It's Funny how things work I mean,
I sit back and watch as the world turns
But yet I'm still lost . . .
Not lost as in physically
But as in spiritually
As I haven't found something
But in my mind I have everything
I mean I have the words of the wise
I have the creativity that any mind would want
But this empty feeling keeps scratching at my mind
And the more the world turns
The more questions fly through my head
But flying is what my mind meant to do
My wings meant to take me free
This thing called being Saker
Is beginning to consume me
Flying away from these questions
Trying to consume my mind
But they will always be their tell the end of time
Painfully True,
Saker

Two Sides

Poetry in MOTION
 Divinity AMONG THE un-awakened
Strength in the UNKNOWN
    AND faith in THE UNFORGOTTEN,
For if we FORGET our past
  We shall lose sight of OUR FUTURE
BUT our future is HOLDing hands with THE PRESENT
    Bounded BY a bond unrecognizable
To THE EYES OF THE human SOUL,
These eyes WHICH only FOCUS on the here and now
They don't look far enough FORWARD
    AND never LOOKS BACK at the shadows of the past
For the past is only forgotten LONG ENOUGH TO REALIZE
    ITS memory
      And its HOPES, DREAMS, AND INSPIRATIONS . . .
But I believe we are BOUND BY FAITH
That keeps us IN the present
And our BELIEF keeps or past with us
Which in the end creates the future? OR AM I
JUST A LOST SOUL dwelling in the past of my future
Which leaves me CAUGHT IN THE PRESENT?

Pinfully True,
SAKER

No Poetry

No poetry was written
No fairytales were read . . .
No color filled the world
Because no vivid words were said
No lives were saved
No souls were touched
Because words bearded no hope
No minds where opened
No songs were made
Because no one made a rhyme
And when there's no music
There is no cheer
So theirs is frowning all the time
And because of wisdom
Words do bear weight
So to change this world
I write my lines with faith
So poetry is my hope . . .
And my words are my weapons
To fight against this unforeseen
Lesson
Or shall I say villain
That we call fear
Because being afraid and sad
Can catch to who is near
So I write with hope and I speak
With Faith,
So I can bring us out of
This forgettable place . . .

Painfully True,
SAKER

Creating

Words are creating,
They can make this world spin and start shaking
Truth be told these words are an art forsaken
Light on the tongue but heavy on the mind
Our words set us free,
Let alone set us up for what we are meant to be
Pursue my goals, with my words I'll pay each toll
My words travel through time teaching
People through rhymes
And Ending wars with each line
Therefore inciting peace, should I embrace these words?
Like I embrace you?
Too show you my visions which start traditions
And watch as worldly dreams come true,
View Sentences written only spoken with truth
And no limited dimensions,
Open minds with words which
Are other dimensions with all this attention?
I only speak to unravel
Your mind wrapped up
Which starts
This so call resurrection of thoughts
And in turn is a progression of a generation once sought
A dream that can't be bought
Motivation birthed by words
This won't be something that goes unheard
See because only the ignorant call
My side of the generation nerds
But what they fail to see is what
Can't be heard it can only be seen
Through the eyes of faith
And a child of imagination
Because this is how true ideas
Are soon created
SO words are Creation . . . .
Painfully True,
Saker

8   *Brandon "Saker" Doyle*

New Beginging

If I listen to the whispers of
    Humanity then I will only live in
        Pain,
But if I follow the whispers
        Of the trees
      Then it shell lead me to the destiny
   Where I am supposed to be . . .
    So with the beat of my heart
      At one with my mind
     The whispers of humanity shall
    Disappear with time
      And in this time
    I shall not be alone in
      This New Beginning
        Which I used to travel alone . . .
               Painfully True,
                Saker

My Mind

Most people want to know
What goes on?
In my mind
But will they truly understand
That every letter
Of every word
I speak Floats around
Freely
In My Mind
Inciting my imagination
And placing me trance
Giving me the look of lost
So here i stand
In my own Mind
Giving you insight
On the incomplete works
Of a bleeding heart and soul . . .
Yet In My Mind
Poetry seems to make me whole . . .

Painfully True,
SAKER

Brandon "Saker" Doyle

Moments

If life were to be broken down
It would be broken down into moments
The moments of joy and laughter that you will forever retain
The few moments of pain and sorrow which you Dred to remember
The moments of lust which you want again and again
The moment of true happiness where you fell nothing can bring you down
And the moment of true love that you know you've found that one person
That completes our life
That one person that gives you all these moments
For a life time in one sitting
And with all these moments like sand
In your hour glass
Falling gracefully into your life
Hoping you never have to tip it over again

PAINFULLY TRUE,
SAKER

Mirrors

Looking into Mirrors
   Seem scary to me
Because my mind is not ready
    For what it might see . . .
It might see the truths
That I need to see
     Or it might see the lies
    Those others want me to see
Because I see three and it's you and it's me
    But I also see the other me
       That no one wants me to see . . .
    Because it might be the truths
That I need to see
     Or it might be the lies
    Those others want me to speak
For to speak the unspoken
    Is to converse with the Wise . . .
    But to even take those first steps
I would have to look into my own eyes
So to look into a Mirror
    Again I must say
      It scares me down to my
    Bones in a very chilling way
Because looking for the truth
    Can only start in one's eyes . . .
So before we can even see
    We must sift through
    The tainted lies . . .
So for now we can only
    Avoid all our fears
     And pray for the strength
To steer us clear of the tainted
    Images our minds seem
    To keep . . .
So stare into

Brandon "Saker" Doyle

These mirrors until you find
Peace in what you see
Because it might be the truths that we all
Need to see
Or it might be the lies that
Others want us to see . . .
Because its pain and its love
And it's a struggle to survive
So in the end we all need to look
Into each other's eyes
And fight away all the shadows
Of hate . . .
And scrape away the lies from our Fate . . .
Before it consumes all of the light
That's left in our lives
Because in the and mirrors
Reflect truth . . .
Because they know the truths
That we need to see
And they show us the lies that others
Want us to believe . . .

Painfully True,
SAKER

Lost

The worst thing to hear about your self
Is being lost
Because you can feel it
You can't hide it because
Your emotions show on your face
You try to fight it but it consumes you more and more
Whispering to you
The more you fight the louder it gets
Tell it's the only thing you hear
Making you question your self
. . . What am i doing . . . .
Is this me . . . I mean really me
I mean I know I lost my
Soul but my heart still stands
Like a one man band still
Beating strong like a Champion
But does it matter when your mind is consumed by this
Thing we call being LOST? . . .

Painfully True,
SAKER

        Brandon "Saker" Doyle

True Feelings

This feeling I get is unlike any other
> Warm but yet cold
>> Strong but yet weak
> Good but yet bad
>>> Wrong but yet right
>> It has my body is a daze, contesting everything it knows
>> It flows through my body intertwined with

With the rivers of my blood
>> Conjoined with every cell so I feel it very well
>>> This sensation that I'm feeling
>> Is brought on by P.A.I.N but yet happiness
>>> Made stronger by anger but deepened by sadness
>>> Yet the more I am around you
> The more the feeling changes

And rearranges with my feelings of love for you

The Girl I mean Woman of my dreams
> The woman that has saved me from myself my times
> The woman who stuck by me even with
>> My faults and Stupidity
>>> So I fear that when I am near you
>>>> My body shall react with this feeling
>> So pure that when I am near you

I finally see clear that my love for you
> Reaches into eternity and back
> Touching my heart that if we were ever apart
> I would be lost not knowing where to start

So I sit here on one knee hoping u would make me

The happiest man and become my wife to be

> > > > Painfully True,
> > > > SAKER

Her Eyes

Your eyes
    Could look at me and pierce through my soul
        But also with warmth on a day I was down
      Your smile could brighten up even the darkest of days cause
        At least I knew you were happy
       Your personality well was the kind that fits you well
     But even with all this said I'll miss you all then same
     Forever a friend up close
        But will like you from afar
       Only without courage because you're such a star
     Your one and a million well I really mean trillion
So what's the worst that can happen, we be friends tell a billion?

                              Painfully True,
                              SAKER

Brandon "Saker" Doyle

A Deeper Look

Look into my eyes
  And watch as the innocents
Washes away
  And the pain takes over
    As I watch
  The love disappears
And the hate boils over
    And the calmness slips away
  And becomes rage
    And with each second
    That passes i am
  I am losing my self-more and more
Being swallowed by this wave of emotions
    Is this when I finally lose myself?
      Am I at that final breaking point?
    But as I ask these questions
  I begin to shake
    And my mind begins to rattle
  I am on the peak of an emotional
    Explosion
  But in the presence of her
  It all goes away
        But I can no longer hold it in
      I have to release my emotions soon
    Because if I don't the troubles will continue
  And my true happiness will never begin
                                    Painfully True,
                                        Saker

Lessons

A wise man once asked
    Why do you seem so immature?
    The man replied to him
Lessons learned is a wiser life lived
    Said the immature man
As the wise man asked
    Why do you walk so are carefree?
  Because if you live with
      Stresses then you become Immature and old
    And none the wiser
      But if you carry on with a nature
    That induces learning than and only then
shall you become a man more the wiser
      So to be truly immature is to not except the lessons
  Of life
But to live and learn
        Where ever your mistakes take you
  Now that is truly living
      The life of the Wise . . .

Painfully True,
SAKER

Brandon "Saker" Doyle

Distant Friends

In a not so far future
  Brought together with strong
 Words that bind them
   These words can open doors
  To a brighter future for them
 Because the words make them stronger
   But also can shut doors to
  By the use of no words
   But to me the act of them
    Saying no words is stronger
 Because the act of speechlessness
Involves trust
It involves knowing the unsaid words
 Front to back like
  A song or book
 But in then end these unsaid words
  Don't make us friends it makes us family
         Painfully True,
         Saker

A S.A.K.E.R.S Feather

Wings Flapping
     Feathers falling
My mind quickly soars away,
        People look into the sky and see nothing
Only feathers that have been
            Left to float away
  In the river that my mind plays in,
          But when these feathers are touched
My pain is reveled, only leaving them in tears
                From the legend I've concealed
          Hearing every word that I don't speak
As they pick up my feathers,
  They go around collecting them
Like they are secret letters
  To understand my legacy
Through the poems, I mean feathers
  That I leave in my wake
Or shall I say the unbeaten path
            My soul seems to take
To fly through the clouds of my own complex mind
      Until I connect the soul that was once mine
        So until that day my feathers will still fall,
My thoughts in the river
  As my mind plays in the sky
A SAKER through and through I shall be
              Tell I die . . . .
                        Painfully True,
                        SAKER

Brandon "Saker" Doyle

One Too Many

One too many losses
  One too many faults
By the time I'm done with
    This poem you'll know what's in my heart
And know it's not a song
  And defiantly not a rap
But my heart beats to rhythm
  But it's not a simple tap
And no it's not a thud
    It sounds something like a hum
      To the rhythm of a clap
      Or could it be a buzz
      A hum, a clap, a buzz?
    See and here comes the problem
    My rhythms out of whack
So the beat in my heart doesn't flow to my head
    Which intern doesn't let my ideas?
Flow to the lead of this pencil
  Or shall I say ink which is
  Is in collaboration
    With my soul
      Which is lost to the rhythm . . . ?
    Of the cluster hearted mind
        Intentions of a soulless
            Body caught in a daze
                  Of my fallen mind
              Crippled trying to rescue my own soul
        Forever falling into this deep thought
          And becoming SAKER forever more . . .
                    Painfully True,
                    Saker

Now I See

I pencil you into this dream of mine
But all that is a dream
That isn't true
All that is true
Is a dream
So while I'm dreaming
Hoping these nightmares i see
Vanish like the thoughts
Of a inconsistently
But consistently i perceive
See that I convert back to
What my mind meant
To see that
I've died and come back to life
I've lived and have not been free
I've starved but never been hungry
but yet and still in the end
i don't stand at the gates of heaven or hell
i stand in front of myself the worst enemy of them all
And that dream i know is true
But what I see isn't me just the shell
    Of something that I wishes to not be
      The only thing that is a reminder of
        Of how I once used to be
          So now that I have grown
      And can see more truthful ways
        I shall follow the path
          That can take me back to
        The start of my broken ways
          So I can live once again
         On a truthful path in life
          But it will never know what path
            Is truly write
             So I will walk until I can't
           And I will fly until I'm free
             And this is the only way
           I shall truly be me
                Painfully True,
                Saker

Brandon "Saker" Doyle

Power

Do you know what power is?
Cause I do
I know that power isn't just the money and the fame
It's not the Notoriety in the things you see
It's the accomplishments in the things you dont see
Or hear
It's the words that you speak from your heart
And the knowledge growing in your mind
And the emotions that leek from your soul
Power isn't material
it's just you and your raw untapped potential . . .
Painfully True,
SAKER

Simplest

People say that poetry is cute
Well ill show you cute
I mean think about it
Saying poetry is cute
Is like saying the love of
Your life is cute . . .
Just those four simple letters
Can take something so amazing
And turn it into something
Average and everyday . . .
And become so mundane that
It washes away
Into the wind trying to cling to
Its True Reality . . .
So with every letter spoken
To form a word
And that word
Into an idea
And with each idea
Used to form a reality
I have learned that
Even the simplest
Words can affect The Soul,
The Mind,
And The Heart . . .

Painfully True,
Saker

Wisdom And Faith

I'll show you what the soul is
Even though I don't have mine
Once you find your soul
You will dance with it forever through time
Witch both has no answers
To this mystery
Of a significant life
But your soul is bounded to your
Bone
This is bounded to your mind
But our soul is the only true answers
To this question we call time . . .
And those who question the soul
Will forever feel my pain . . .
But not to many people
Have my power . . .
Over the words
That touches the soul
And makes a person
True and Whole . . .

With Wisdom and Faith,
SAKER

Whispers

The secrets in life
We can't answers
But the answers are right in our face
Yet we ignore them like we do
Problems we don't want to handle
This world is so fast paced
We never stop and listen
I mean truly listen
I mean the earth talks
Just like the wind and the trees but the only
Answers we give back is destruction and mayhem
So without answers we live lost
As a kind and a whole
But I for one am listening
Still searching for each whisper
Without regrets or remorse
Painfully True,
SAKER

Pain 11

what is pain?
    Is it the body
  Reaching its breaking point?
      or is it a defense mechanism?
   Maybe it's the soul touching
        Your mind
        And bypassing you conscience
        Maybe it's the realization
           Of how small we are to the world
          I mean think about it
          Do we really know this world?
          This world that pain frequents more than death
           So is pain beyond death
             Or shall I say more powerful?
           But that still leaves the question
            What is pain?

With wisdom and Faith,
SAKER

Tormented

I've been fighting them forever
  Or what seems like ages
    Before I was even born
      My demons broke from their cages . . .
And caused me plenty of anguish
  And made me angry and such
Before I thought they were undefeatable
  But I learned secrets and such
  They're not just in my mind
  They are in the minds of many
These Tormented Demons
    Are undefeatable to plenty
But they don't have my knowledge
  So they are scared of their own minds
      They never search for answers
So the demons spread over time
          Like a cancer they stick
      But I'm here to give you hope
And this defiantly is a dream
          And for sure isn't a joke
I'll give you all my wisdom
    Courtesy of my tormented dreams
      The answers are in your mind
You just have to find your soul
  This is the ultimate weapon
      And you will soon feel whole . . .

Painfully True,
SAKER

Brandon "Saker" Doyle

Our World

This world
  So small of the mind
  Yet the only thing that last
      Thought the centuries
        Is time and words
      Or shall I timeless words
    Words spoken endlessly
          Over the days, months, and years
          Each word said to have simple meanings
  Unchangeable by time or even us human beings
        But every word spoken
          By even the person of simplest hearts
Shall change the definition
        Even if said by the purest of hearts
      And the darkest of souls
          But every word spoken makes that being feel like it is whole
      So if you think about words
            Even the simplest like one
              It has 6 billion definitions
            And you thought it was just number 1
        So open your mind to the vast knowledge
              In your heart
                The key is in your mind
                      I'll show you where to start
              Step into my world
                  And let the words flow freely
                6 billion definitions
                      But mine make it easy . . .
                          Painfully True,
                            Saker

To Taste Words

As the words begin
    To formulate
   i begin to taste each letter . . .
    But as they come out it's like
     i could have truly found something better

  I don't know about you but
    I don't like the way poetry sounds
   It's like you're always forced to rhyme
    SO let's go for the unconventional now
   See because the words taste so sweet
    Like a fresh fruit in the spring

    But it floats into your mind
     Thought the whispers of the trees
    Then with is condolences of the
     Night and its wavering stars
      It seems to come for a different time
     Like the city lights from afar

SO as I said before Poetry sounds wrong
But the words taste so sweet

So as I begging to write them
I let the wisdom set into their ink
As it radiates the words with life
But my thoughts seem to be birds
Always moving fast as the wings of humming birds
Moving to touch the world flowery hearts
And cure the seas of sadness

Yes in a poets mind seem to be
Some mismatched madness
So with my crooked smile
I will tell you what is true to me
I don't like the way it sounds just poetry to me
But the words are so sweet that
I will forever write
To fuel my mind in this
Crazy realm we call life . . . .

Painfully True,
SAKER

Souls

What do Souls Want?
Is it fame or Glory?
Love or Joy beyond its host wildest dreams?
. . . I could keep going
Making every question toward
The Seven Deadly sins
The ones our humanly nature
Always fall to
But I believe its fate
Undeniable, and unchanging
I believe I know what they want
They want to be heard
And felt, not just spiritually
But physically,
They want to be found
They want their true host
Not only to hear their conscience
But to hear the soul speak to them
And to guide them to their true selves
But in the end the true question is what do you want?
Painfully True,
Saker

Brandon "Saker" Doyle

Simply Life

With Every Stroke of my pen
I speak on life,
Words and the soul,
But this one thing is
All I can do to feel whole . . .
On the outside I show face
But on the inside my body
Rattles and Shakes my mind
And it's hard to live
When you feel this way
All the time . . .
So with each word I rhyme
The feeling of lonely
Slips away with each line
Or design
And the shaking Slows
To just a heart beat
SO with every Beat of Life
I become mesmerized with
The stroke of the pen
Of which I write
And this is simply
What i call
LIFE . . .
Painfully True,
SAKER

New Beginning

If I listen to the whispers of
    Humanity then I will only live in
        Pain,
But if it follow the whispers
        Of the trees
        Then it shell lead me to the destiny
    Where i am supposed to be . . .
      So with the beat of my heart
        At one with my mind
        The whispers of humanity shall
     Disappear with time
          And in this time
       I shall not be alone in
         This New Beginning
            Which I used to travel alone . . .
                Painfully True,
                Saker

Brandon "Saker" Doyle

Life

Four simple letters
Life
That make up a word that's
So big
We truly don't understand it
I'm mean think about it
When the word is spoken
It's simply meant for the living
But we don't take into account
That in tales breathing,
Thinking,
Interacting,
And anything else life
I mean LIFE touches
I mean you almost have to shout it
LIFE!
Just four simple letters
That touches your heart and soul
But yet our minds can't fully comprehend
These four simple letters
Painfully True,
Saker

The Fallen

Fallen Angel
    Demon warrior
   Revolving around a single cause
Bounded by instincts driven
   Far beyond the Ancient
But still questioning the beginning
   Or shall I say the Alpha
  This insinuates there is an end
   Or an Omega of such
But this insights a question,
    Why does this instinct feel so unrelenting?
     This instinct that touches life and death
   That traps Spirits and ghost
  That forms good and evil
    But who is to tell what's good
     And what's evil
    That line between good and evil
     Has been drawn but no one remembers who
      Or what did it
     Let alone know the true definition
      Of Good & Evil . . .
        Painfully True,
        Saker

Broken Faith

I am, I was, and I will forever be . . .
Nothing more . . .
Nothing more
Than a lost cause . . .
So . . . Why,
Why . . . Feel . . .
Why have emotions
What's the point . . .
This, this feeling is worse
Than feeling lost
For at least feeling lost you have
. . . hope . . .
And right now i don't even have faith
But even faith is nothing more
Than hopes little brother
So what does that leave me with?
Belief . . .
Now that is something
We all need
Even still I have nothing to believe in
Besides my own words
So with all my words
I shall live by imagination

Painfully True,

Saker

The Four Roses

The *White* rose is for the wind
Who is bitter liker the winter
        But cool in the relaxing days off
The *Yellow* rose is for my Friends
        Who are everything and more?
Throughout my life and summer days
            The *Black* rose is for my aunt
                Who I love
Who has died and passed on
Like the leaves of the fall
            And the *Purple* rose
For you who is like spring
        Bringing happiness and joy
To those around you
        Putting a smile on everyone's face
You the fourth an most special rose
    The rose I keep closest to my heart

                    Painfully True,
                    Saker

Brandon "Saker" Doyle

Life Is Like

Life reminds me of a card trick
I learned
It has a little bit of This
This being the memories brought close to your mind
It has a little bit of That
That being the memories that take a thought or more to understand
And not much of The Other
The other being the things our eyes tend not to recognize
Until it is brought to our attention
Or a closer incitement is brought upon us
So until our life is lived with full awareness
Our soul is touched with
A little bit of THIS
A little bit of THAT
And not much of THE OTHER
Painfully True,
SAKER

Finialy Found

Finally Found
   Finally heard
  For once i can hear
Those unspoken words
   For they are the truth
  Amongst all the lies
And all of the disrespectful
     Eyes . . .
   So in this world of
  Unforeseen Truths
    We can only live by
    What we seek inside our
     Own mind
     And find those
       Unspoken words
    For in them is only the
Truth that we all subconsciously
     Seek . . .
     And what we seek
Is what we should always speak
     So now that i have thought
    And my words are being formed
  I shall speak on what was
     What is?
  And what shall always
  Be me . . .
         Painfully True,
          Saker

Brandon "Saker" Doyle

(Untitled)

In life one thing I've learned
Is that words impact people
More than what is lead on to believe . . .
I mean me personally
Have more than just faith in them
I believe that words don't just touch the mind
But they also touch the soul
So with words
Bearing this great power
To travel from one mind
To another's soul . . .
I can only think
That this only bears
A true burden on ones emotions
For ones emotions is the true tie
From the Heart Mind and Soul
So, for every word I speak
Shall be true,
So my heart and my mind
Shall feel my faith in words as i
Speak to you . . .
And my belief in words shall always say true
So this is what makes me different form you . . .
My words are focused to touch ones soul
So one day i can fill that empty whole
And help the next person to find Soul . . .
So forever a S.A.K.E.R I am to you
But with my words I shall always stay true . . .
Painfully True,
SAKER

I Never Know

I never know what to say . . . but . . .
There is this woman . . .
I smile from just seeing her name . . .
Her presence stops my heart and stops it again . . .
When she is around i smile but her absence leaves my mind to wonder . . .
Daydreaming about her and all her sweetness . . .
Her laugh
Her smile
Her personality just picks me up when I'm down . . .
I mean i never know what to say . . .
Not trying to pressure her in any way . . .
But the truth is she is on my mind . . . I as a friend want to think of her as mine . . .
And me as her's because she's just simply amazing . . .
Wondering if she will ever know my true feelings . . . true and unchanged
Tired of sitting back and watching . . . Here i am in the open, my feelings out on this page
Never again to be trapped in a cage, I speak them true . . . I hope when she is done reading this
She knows that i am true,
The truth shall set me free . . .
And now it's off my chest . . .
I hope this poem will help with the rest . . .

Painfully True,
Saker

Coming Home

I'm on my way home
And my mind is in a trance
My heart is in my body doing its happy dance
My soul has gone away
It's already done
It's already home
It said too much pain I'm DONE!
But home is a vague definition
Is home where your heart is?
Cause mine is chained to my chest
To move with me like the bear a little kid clenches to his knees
Or is home where your soul is to forever be laid to rest
But I say home is to be happy
Home is to be free
Home is where the soul and the heart is at ease
So I shall take my flight
And let my heart and mind be one
My home is with my soul
And once I find it I am done . . . .
Painfully True,
Saker

When I

When I cry I cry blood from the pain that I have cause her,
   When I bleed I bleed tears because I've shed so many over
What I have lost and how good it was,
when I'm awake I dream nightmares hoping it's not real,
            When I sleep its reality setting in . . . .
. . . . without her my life is a mess . . .
            Destined to be a SAKER forever more . . . .
   And now that I have my wings
            I shall fly until the scene is green
   Cause all I want to do is smile
               But without her it might be awhile
   I will fly until I'm close to space
               To awaken from this deep dark place . . .

Painfully True,
Saker

Brandon "Saker" Doyle

Loveless

For is had lost love
. . . and when i first met you,
    I never would have imagined that i would have
        Such strong feelings for you.
I never would have thought that
I would have dreams about you or miss
Being by your side or getting butterflies in my stomach
        When someone mentions your name.
When I first met you i never would've thought that i would fall for you.
. . . you who's soul is attached to mine because
Our love is intertwined . . . until I meet you again I'm just
Another lost soul wondering . . .
        Waiting for that moment when
        Everything makes sense . . . .
            When that one person can complete
            What soul I have left
            And make me feel like nothing else matters
                For when I first meet you
        My soul will begin to shape
            And my mind will want to make
        Every moment in every second matter
                                    Painfully True,
                                    Saker

Enlightenment

To become Aware
Is to live by the
Letters of every word you speak
And to Speak upon
Every Letter that Formulates
In your mind
Because once you've tapped
Into your most
"INNER SELF"
Every letter in every word
You Speak shall
Be spoken from your soul
And once your soul
Becomes one with your Mind . . .
And Your Mind becomes one
With your Heart
You will truly become . . .
AWARE . . .
Painfully True,
SAKER

Brandon "Saker" Doyle

This Is

This is Poetry
This is Soul
This is what it's like to feel whole
This is Love
This is Life
This is the only thing that makes me feel alright
This is faith
This is Friends
This is the only good thing I can do with a pen
So Step into my mind
So you can hear my truths
And Now that I am a Saker
I can fly for the skies
Because as of now
My words will not die
They will stick into your minds
And help you find yourself
I do this out of love and not for the wealth
So step into my mind as I begin to sore
and let my imagination take you
To heights unseen . . .

Painfully True,
Saker

For Once I Have Found Faith

Faith in words that is
   For they are the strongest thing in this
      World, they can start wars
     Incite Peace,
        Give hope
          And illustrate emotions
        Each word to me paints a picture
         That connects imaginations from
       Many different corners of the world, but yet
          Our minds interprets in the way
            Only our imagination can understand
          But to understand we must become WISE
           And to be wise we must DREAM
         And with dreams comes a deeper belief in your FAITH . . .
                 Painfully True,
                   Saker

Brandon "Saker" Doyle

Made in the USA
Monee, IL
08 July 2022

99344509R00038